MW00892937

Success Is Spelled with Two C's!

The Average Person's 20-Day Guide & Workbook to

Becoming Successful

JAVAY J. JOHNSON

Success Is Spelled with Two C's!

The Average Person's 20-Day Guide & Workbook to Becoming Successful

By JAVAY J. JOHNSON

Copyright © 2013 Javay Johnson, LLC All rights reserved.

No part of this publication may be reproduced, distributed, or transmitted in any form or by any means, including photocopying, recording, or other electronic or mechanical methods, without the prior written permission of the publisher, except in the case of brief quotations embodied in critical reviews and certain other noncommercial uses permitted by copyright law. For permission requests, please visit www.JavayJohnson.com

The information contained in this book is intended to be educational and not for diagnosis, prescription, or treatment of any health disorder whatsoever. The intent of this book is to provide general information in regard to the subject matter covered. This information should not replace the consultation with your physician or competent healthcare professional. The author and publisher are in no way responsible or liable for any misuse of the material.

Disclaimer: The advice and strategies contained herein may not be suitable for all situations. This work is sold with the understanding that the Author and Publisher are not engaged in rendering legal, accounting, or other professional services. If professional assistance is needed, the services of a competent professional person should be acquired. Neither the Author nor the Publisher shall be liable for damages arising herefrom. The fact that an organization or website is referred to in this work and/or a potential source of further information, does not mean that the Author or Publisher endorses the information the organization or website may provide or recommend. In addition, readers should be aware that the internet sites listed in this work may have changed or become defunct between when this work was written and when it is read.

First Printing, 2013

Library of Congress Control Number: 2013906231

ISBN-13: 978-1483943077
ISBN- 10: 1483943070

PRINTED IN CHARLESTON, SOUTH CAROLINA

Ordering information:
Quantity sales and special discounts are available on quantity purchases by corporations, organizations, associations etc. For details, please contact Javay Johnson via www.JavayJohnson.com

Editors: Rashida Johnson & Ashara Golden
Cover: Jason Taylor

"Dedicated to those

of us who were ever told

that they could not

do whatever 'it' was

and succeed!"

Contents

INTRODUCTION

It is fascinating how certain situations unfold in life. Sometimes what appears to be an inconvenience really turns out to be a blessing in disguise. If you look closely enough, life's bumps in the road are actually cornerstones and building blocks of a much grander picture. I was 18 years old; no job, no credit, no car, and newly labeled "HOMELESS." Growing up in a middle class family, I had no exposure to what it meant not to have a place to rest my head. As I look back in retrospect, 18 can be a very difficult age. You are somewhat grown in respect to responsibility, but if you are still under your parents' roof, it is imperative to abide by their rules. Well, I wanted to make my own rules, and I found myself with no place to call home.

So, how was I to transition into the 'real world'? I needed something that would enable me to become self-sufficient and independent quickly. That quest for independence led me to the Alternative for Girls Shelter located in St. Peters Church on the corner of Michigan Ave. and Trumbull in Detroit, Michigan. I will never forget that day. I arrived broken, fearful, and emotionally drained. I had no clue what to expect, and I did not like the stigma that was associated with being homeless. I remember crying because of the fear of the unknown, and the fact that I, for the first time in my young life, felt like I had hit rock bottom. I believed that I was worthless. I also grew tired of burdening and depending on other family members and close friends. I felt immense guilt because at the end of the day, I was not their responsibility.

Ever since that sad day when I entered the shelter, many of the things that I wanted to accomplish have been achieved. The experience of being homeless is the greatest milestone I have achieved thus far; in fact, it is the foundation for all of my other accomplishments in life.

It is very important to me to share my message of hope throughout *Success Is Spelled with Two C's*. Years ago, while living in the homeless shelter, I knew that I would one day be sharing, encouraging, empowering and liberating someone who needed to hear a *true* story of the journey from "struggle" to success. I knew then that someone in the future would need to hear my testimony of hope. I knew that someone needed to know that they matter. YOU MATTER!

In this vast, infinite universe of seven billion people, your existence actually means something to the world, even if you do not know it yet. Negative incidents and unfavorable circumstances of the past, and what you have been through, do not define you as a person. It is what you do to counteract those negative incidents in an effort to move forward that matters. It is the ability to learn from your past that allows you experience a better now, and a better future.

YOU define YOU. Your plan for the future defines YOU. If you have fallen, what you do after you get back up defines YOU! You are magnificent and your existence is much too great to be limited to the ebb and flow of life's sometimes messy experiences.

> *"An arrow goes forward only after pulling it backwards*
> *A bullet goes forward only after pressing the trigger backward*
> *Every human being will get happy only after facing the difficulties in their life's path*
> *So do not be afraid to face your difficulties*
> *They will push you forward"*
> - Unknown

So, how did I fare living in the homeless shelter? Well, once I realized that I had the power to take control of my life, I simply did it. I set goals, I worked towards the goals until I accomplished them. And month by month my life began to get better. After emotionally regrouping and accepting my circumstances, I got to work…literally. I was given a shot at interviewing for a Unit Clerk/ Telemetry Technician position at a hospital. I received the job. I enrolled into Wayne State University for the fall semester which was covered partially by a scholarship and financial aid. My life consisted of studying, going to work, completing shelter modules and requirements, and having daily conversations with the Creator!

I may have been physically homeless, but as I begin to heal, my home became where my heart was. I started with forgiveness. I first needed to forgive myself, and from that point, I was able to forgive others. I also started pouring positive energy into my own life. I took an hour out of my day to have an uninterrupted conversation with the Creator. With words and feelings of gratitude and humility, I was able to see the divine beauty in my situation. I began to view my life from a positive disposition. I began to make progress with accomplishments, and simply being able to do that made me feel even better and greater each day. The *more* you do, the MORE you do!!!

While writing this book, I was completing my own projects after my corporate career. Although it was often a daunting struggle to find means of financial stability, it also provided a window of opportunity to reflect on my own life. I reflected on where I had been, where I was going, and what must be done to get there. Asking these kinds of questions brings awareness to the core of what life is all about. At one point I thought I knew the answers to those questions. I felt like I used to be ahead of the game, only to realize that I was only at the beginning. The inevitable struggles with faith, self-realization, luck, bad decisions, emotions, pride, self-doubt, etc. brought me to one conclusion; Life… is just life.

True change on the outside begins in the inside. Sometimes having the ability to change your perspective, of your situation, is a determining factor in the outcome quality. If you decide to hold on to failure and defeat, you will begin to attract more failure and defeat into your life. You must not give up on determination because with determination you will be able to overcome seemingly impossible odds.

One day, all that you have learned, endured and sacrificed will be transformed into something so great, that it pushes the boundaries of what the human mind can conceive. This is you, this is me. This is all of us on a quest for a better life.

How can you get positive results in your life? This 20-day guide/workbook has been specially designed in the hope that each and every one of you can have a renewed experience in life at the time of completion. You will be interactively engaged in a journey of introspective reflection while learning life changing dynamics such as; goal setting, budgeting, defining success, shifting your mindset, self-marketing, gratitude, motivation, unveiling resources and more. For you to get the most out of this experience, it is my hope that you complete this guide/workbook with honesty, commitment and the determination to make wonderful, positive changes in your life. As you complete each chapter and its respective journal entries and exercises DAILY, you may find that you will get inspired to tackle projects and tasks that you may have previously procrastinated on because you did not know where to start. So, get prepared to have fun and to learn more than you have ever known about yourself, for this is going to be a splendid journey for you!

TOOLS TO PACK FOR THE JOURNEY

First you will want to have an opened mind! This journey will be full of exciting outcomes of you actually doing the fun work. Worksheets and journal entry pages are provided at the end of each chapter in this 20-day guide/workbook for your convenience. However, a couple of the exercises require the use of some index cards (Chapter: Eighteen), two small poster boards, a monthly wall calendar (Chapter: Two), some magazines, photos, scissors and glue (Chapter: Three). The use of color through markers or pens to customize your small exercise projects is highly recommended but not required.

Journal Question # 1

Who are you at this very moment? Try your best to provide the most accurate description and intimate portrayal of who you are right now. This exercise is very important because it will be revisited as you continue to make significant progress with this guide/workbook's exercises.

_____

_____

_____

_____

_____

_____

_____

_____

_____

_____

_____

_____

_____

_____

_____

CHAPTER ONE: DEFINING SUCCESS

As time progresses and our surroundings continually evolve, so does the idea of success. This is why many people believe that success is more of a journey rather than a permanent destination. Successful people are people on a continuous journey, who maximize beneficial opportunities in the quest for betterment. Once you achieve the success that you have defined, you also have to continue making decisions that will maintain the success that you have achieved.

"To those whom much is given, much is expected." – John F. Kennedy

What exactly is success? Is it a level? Is it a state of mind? Is it a place? Is it an idea? Or shall these questions be rephrased to ask; "How do YOU define success?" Are you defining success for yourself based on what you see around you? Do you define success by other people's interpretation of you? Do you define success as having large amounts of money, fancy cars, a big house, etc.? I used to define success from the perspective described above, and from having that mindset I developed an internal conflict within myself. I had not recognized the multitude of small, yet important, accomplishments that I had made in my life. These small accomplishments are the stepping stones to the path of my success in the grand scheme of things. I used to measure my accomplishments by material gains that intrinsically did not matter!

Success is an energy, a frequency, a vibration, and a wave; to the likeness of an ocean tidal wave. When surfers catch a wave, their entire intent is to resiliently ride that wave until they can ride it no longer. You can see success on people, and it has nothing to do with the clothes that they are wearing. You can smell it, but it is not the perfume or cologne. It is a full embodiment of energy that surrounds successful people and it emanates throughout their speech, their demeanor, posture and more. There is a certain confidence, or some may call it 'swag' about the person. Successful people can tip-toe into a crowded room of strangers, but their presence is so thunderous, that everyone in the room acknowledges that this person is there. When you carry a successful vibration, your existence is indelible. When people come up to you and say they remember you from somewhere; that means you left a lasting impression. Think about it, there are 7 billion people in the world today and someone remembered *you*.

If you are in pursuit of a dream, what better person than you, can give you credit, validate you and praise you? After all, if you are not willing to do this for yourself, then how do you expect others to appreciate your contributions to the world? Let's look at an example of a person who believes that their purpose in life is to become a famous singer. This singer has worked very hard to secure a major recording label deal, and has chosen to define their idea of success by means of notoriety, money and the lifestyle of fame. On the local level, within the singer's hometown, the singer has performed at quite a few venues, and has begun to create a realm of local recognition. How many people need to know the singer, before he/she can be labeled as famous? How much money does the singer need in order to reach this status of 'fame'? How many people are needed to sing the lines of the singer's songs before that singer can believe that he or she is a STAR?

Many of us look for success on the outside. You will never find it there. True success begins within. You must believe that you are already successful. Own the vision and idea of what you want to become in the future. Many times we define ourselves by standards that are set by others such as industry standards, academic standards, financial standards, parental standards, etc. Ponder for a moment the idea of not having any external pre-set standards to measure ourselves against. Would we simply live as individuals accepting ourselves for who we are in a world where motivations and decisions stem directly from what makes us feel good and happy inside? What if every person in this world contributed a talent that was solely and uniquely different, that fueled vital and essential roles in the existence of humanity? Perhaps the focal point of mediocrity or excellence would be you. You would be the only person in the world who could perform an isolated talent. Whether it is performed well or not would only be open to judgment by you. If there is no other talent to compare, then you would in fact be your own standard of what greatness is.

In order to keep an unadulterated focus on your success, sometimes you may have to create a protective realm around you. I like the idea of mentally creating what I call a 'safety tunnel'. This 'safety tunnel' can be mentally designed and decorated however you want it to be. This tunnel is a place where you can go, and where there is no one there *but* you. It is a place where you can continue to work on yourself, your goals or your dreams without the interruption of external stimuli such as negative chatter and opinions. This tunnel protects you from the unwanted opinions, criticisms, and negativity commonly accompanied with the pursuit of success. Although it seems realistic that your closest counterparts should support what you do, it is not uncommon to receive the greatest amount of resistance, push back and lack of support from those close to you. The reasons for lack of support may vary, and though some of it may be sincere concern with your best interest at heart, be prepared to filter all responses sifting the destructive from the constructive. If this is not a reality for you, then of course it is a good thing. Support is a great tool to encourage you to do your best. With or without encouragement, the ideal way to operate in the world of manifesting your goals is to do so independent of the opinions of others. As with much criticism, remember it is more than likely just an opinion, so do not absorb it too personally without examining if and how it can work to your benefit. More on this later!

Consider this scenario: a decorated war veteran, who has fought for his country, rising above basic expectations, sacrifice and bravery, is now back in the U.S. and is now unfortunately homeless. Is not this decorated war veteran still a hero, measured by his/her accomplishments regardless of their current status? Based on your own standards, if you believe that you are a hero for something that you have done in life for the betterment of someone, something, or a situation, then you are a hero, even if you receive absolutely no recognition for your deed. The unseen hero lies within us all, and validation of that is not from a newspaper article, a televised interview, or monetary reward. The choice is yours, who are you *not* to be great or successful? Who are you *not* to be able to define your own success?

<u>Journal Question # 2</u>

What is your personal definition of success? This answer should be your personal view, not the world's view, television's view or your peers view.

_____

_____

_____

_____

_____

_____

_____

_____

_____

_____

_____

_____

_____

_____

_____

_____

_____

_____

_____

_____

_____

Exercise #1

Let's tap into that wonderful vibration of success! Adapting the ideology that success is not solely based upon monetary compensation, please list 15 reasons why you are currently successful. When completed, review this list daily, so that you can build up and reinforce success in your life. (Page 17)

I AM SUCCESSFUL BECAUSE...

1._____

2._____

3._____

4._____

5._____

6._____

7._____

8._____

9._____

10._____

11._____

12._____

13._____

14._____

15._____

16._____

17._____

18._____

19._____

20._____

<u>Exercise #2</u>

Create a 'Negative Thought Equalizer List'. Write out several accomplishments and achievements, that you have made from childhood up until your current age. Whenever you feel discouraged, retrieve this 'Negative Thought Equalizer List' as a reminder of the obstacles you have overcome, and the great things you have achieved. (Page 19)

NEGATIVE THOUGHT EQUALIZER LIST

1._____

2._____

3._____

4._____

5._____

6._____

7._____

8._____

9._____

10._____

11._____

12._____

13._____

14._____

15._____

16._____

17._____

18_____

19._____

20._____

CHAPTER TWO: SUCCESS ANALOGY

I liken the journey of success synonymously to driving a vehicle with a standard manual transmission, commonly called a stick shift. With standard manual transmissions, there are five gears which enable you to shift and accelerate from low to high speeds and downshift to lower gears and speeds. In addition to the five gears there is a neutral and reverse position on the shifter. In order to accelerate, you have to change gears. Let's look at the methodology of shifting into first gear to put the vehicle into forward motion.

Imagine that you are at a red stop light at the intersection of Success Blvd. and Hindrance Way. You are waiting to proceed North on Success Boulevard with your trusty, reliable vehicle. The gear shifter is in neutral, and you have your right foot on the brake pedal. The light turns green, you press on the clutch pedal while moving the gear shifter into first gear and then apply pressure to the gas pedal. You accelerate! Those who drive a manual 5-speed transmission already know what happens if you don't properly balance out the pressure of your feet on the clutch pedal and the gas pedal! Improper balancing will cause the vehicle to jerk and in some cases temporarily stall. This mechanical example works the same way with one's quest to become successful.

The vehicle is your trusty, reliable plan of action on the Success Boulevard. Gears one through five are your opportunities on hand that can either speed up your plan of action, or slow down your plan of action. The gas pedal is your drive, persistence, and resilience. The brake pedal helps you to slow down to see the big picture when your plan is moving too fast. The clutch pedal is the medium to help you make a smooth transition from one goal to the next within your plan of action. If your drive, persistence, and resilience (gas pedal) is not balanced out with the medium to help you make a smooth transition from one goal to the next (clutch pedal), then at the intersection of Success Boulevard and Hindrance Way, your vehicle is going to jerk, lurch, grind and stall out! Your trusty, reliable plan of action is once again at a halt, and only just a few feet away from where you started. I have found myself at this intersection many times, sitting there stalled out. I have wanted to go straight from neutral into fifth gear. The reality is that the gears work in numerical order, and sometimes, we may find ourselves with our gear shifter all out of order, with burnt out clutches.

You have this ingenious idea, you think that you have perfected the plan to make the idea reality, and out of nowhere a road block appears. Now that road block can be permanent or temporary, and that depends on the ingenuity of the navigator. As a navigator, are you willing to put your vehicle in reverse to take a different route? Are you fully knowledgeable of other routes that can bypass the road blocks? Do you have an emergency assistance service that can tow you away from adverse road conditions? It does not matter how fool proof you think your plan is. There may always be that variable lurking within the formula that just simply is not accounted for. That is why it is a good idea to construct more than one plan, because you may have to detour your route in order to successfully arrive at your destination.

Journal Question #3

What are some obstacles that you have overcome to achieve your goals? What obstacles are still in your way that you need to remove or maneuver around to achieve success?

_____

_____

_____

_____

_____

_____

_____

_____

_____

_____

_____

_____

_____

_____

_____

_____

_____

_____

_____

_____

Exercise #3

Before you devise a plan, you must have goals in mind that you seek to accomplish. A goal is an aim, intention or purpose that typically has a start date and a completion date, and commonly involves a celebration when it is accomplished! List ten (10) long term goals that you would like to accomplish in the next five (5) years on the bolded line. Now using the ten (10) long term goals, for each one write out five (5) short term goals on the indented lines, that you can complete in one (1) year or less that will aid in the completion of each of your long term goals. (Pages 24-27)

LONG & SHORT TERM GOALS

1._____

    1._____

    2._____

    3._____

    4._____

    5._____

2._____

    1._____

    2._____

    3._____

    4._____

    5._____

3._____

    1._____

    2._____

    3._____

    4._____

    5._____

4. _____

    1. _____

    2. _____

    3. _____

    4. _____

    5. _____

5. _____

    1. _____

    2. _____

    3. _____

    4. _____

    5. _____

6. _____

    1. _____

    2. _____

    3. _____

    4. _____

    5. _____

7. _____

    1. _____

    2. _____

    3. _____

    4. _____

    5. _____

8. _____

    1. _____

    2. _____

    3. _____

    4. _____

    5. _____

9. _____

    1. _____

    2. _____

    3. _____

    4. _____

    5. _____

10. _____

    1. _____

    2. _____

    3. _____

    4. _____

    5. _____

Exercise #4

Create a monthly goal board for the next calendar month. Using a poster board, affix a calendar month page to the right side of the poster board. (You can Google: 'Monthly Calendar Page' or use an existing calendar that has space for you to write in the daily boxes.) Using the list of short term goals, make a **new** list of goals that will help you to accomplish your short term goals on the left side of the poster board. The new goals should be micro-goals that can be accomplished in 30 days or less, and that will move you forward in completing your short term goals. Next, number each of the goals listed on the left side of the poster board. Use the numbers of the goals and write it on a specific day on your calendar to denote when you want to have that specific goal completed. Continue this process until you have transferred all of the number representations of each goal to the calendar month page.

CHAPTER THREE: WHOSE PURPOSE IS IT ANYWAY?

What is your purpose? How would you define yourself? What are YOU all about? What are your goals? What are you passionate about? What do you hope to achieve in your life? It is a good idea at some point in your life to do a self-assessment. You can find many free online personality profiles and career assessments online. By taking an assessment, you can get a general idea about what you may, or may not want to do with your life. Believe it or not, but personality profiles are really good for measuring and determining if you have the right personality traits to be successful in certain roles. Finding the proper match between a career and your personality can save you time, stress, and you will be making educated decisions that can potentially propel you further in life. Just because a job title sounds interesting to you, it does not mean that you will excel in that position.

Another, a great idea is to develop a personal mission statement. Successful Fortune 500 companies have mission statements so why shouldn't you? A mission statement is a summary of the goals, aims, and values of a company, organization, or individual. Having a mission statement is very helpful for organizing your core values. Once you have identified what you value in life, it is much easier to use your completed mission statement as a guide in creating new opportunities for yourself and to ensure that new opportunities are aligned with your mission.

Journal Question #4

Which scenario would you prefer; work to get paid or to be compensated for your passion? Take this moment right now and think about what you are passionate about. What would you rather be doing in life? Be as descriptive as possible.

_____

_____

_____

_____

_____

_____

_____

_____

_____

_____

_____

_____

_____

_____

_____

_____

_____

Exercise #5

Write your own mission statement. Read it daily to reinforce who you are and what you believe your purpose is. (Page 32)

THE MISSION STATEMENT OF_____

_____

_____

_____

_____

_____

_____

_____

_____

_____

Exercise #6

Create what is called a 'vision board' and display it in a place where you are able to see it daily. Use your written mission statement as a guide to find images and word representations of what you would like to achieve out of life, and affix them to a poster board. You are also encouraged to use pictures of yourself, family, friends, and any other positive images from magazines. The selection of items can represent the following categories:

- ✓ Faith
- ✓ Health
- ✓ Family
- ✓ Wealth

- ✓ Love
- ✓ Success
- ✓ Fulfillment

CHAPTER FOUR: BEING EXTRAORDINARY

Being extraordinary is a choice. You can choose to succumb to mediocrity or you can catapult yourself above and beyond average. The choice is ultimately yours. Your thoughts, ideas, words, actions, surroundings, associations, etc. reflects how driven you are to achieve your goals and manifest your dreams. The energy around you, given that you are truly focused on your goals will ultimately shape and plan your unique and great path. Your path will surprisingly roll out for you like a red carpet, day by day, even if you sometimes can't recognize it in front of you.

If you have a true talent, you have an obligation to bring it forth and use it for good! You can impact nothing in this world just by sitting on the sideline. The whole world is waiting for you and what you have to offer! So all of you who are reading this, who are in a dead end job, you are not only doing yourself a disservice by staying there; you are potentially blocking a position for someone else who really needs that job. It is in our divine interest that we live the life we were created for, and realize the potential of who we were created to be. What can you do now to avoid looking back at your life with regrets someday?

Journal Question #5

Who is it that you would hope to have become by the age of 100? Imagining that you are now 100 years old and looking back on your life, what did you accomplish? How many people's lives did you positively affect? What did you contribute to the world? What advice/wisdom do you think you would have to share with young adults?

_____

_____

_____

_____

_____

_____

_____

_____

_____

_____

_____

_____

_____

_____

_____

_____

_____

CHAPTER FIVE: VALLEYS IN LIFE ARE AS COMMON AS THE COMMON COLD

If you are sad, it is okay! Ride it out like it is a common cold! There is no "end-all" cure for sadness. You will have sad moments in your life as you metaphorically travel throughout mountains and fight your way out of the valleys. There is currently no cure for the common cold, but there are certain things that you can do to minimize the aggravating symptoms to make your cold experience more tolerable. Why not view the valleys in life that cause sadness the same way?

When you are a person with a dream, and you are driven to make it a reality, sometimes you will occasionally embark upon the land of sadness. Sometimes this sadness is derived from having unsuccessful attempts at mastering your definition of success. Once you can accept that failure is a part of the on-going process of becoming successful, your understanding of the cycle of sadness will be understood and managed better. In some cases, there is an internal conflict between sadness and the person who is experiencing it. Many times on our path, sadness is not necessarily embraced. After all, who really wants to be gloomy, down or depressed? If we were not human, and did not have emotions, perhaps sadness would not be an issue. However, sadness is nothing different from any other life changing, paradigm shifting, and mind altering situation.

Sadness is also a grieving/cleansing process as well. If you don't take the time to deal with your emotions productively, they will always be lurking in the shadows of your attempts for success. I can remember being fired from a job and then launching my new business and website the very next week. I continued to push on, tackling additional business ventures, as my primary business endeavors were very slow. After a while, I started to feel defeated, which was also a direct effect of my lack of taking the time to grieve, cleanse, re-group and nurture myself after being terminated from my previous job. My goal was to WIN. I was afraid that if I took a second to let the smoke clear emotionally, that my former employer would win; they would have defeated Javay Johnson. I felt that I could not simply lay down on the train tracks to wait for my ultimate demise. This is why you should not allow perceived rejection to affect your self-perception. Every decision that is made is not always personal. For months I believed that I was terminated from my job because my boss simply did not like me. The reality was that I was not performing in my position at an acceptable level per the company's standard. That decision had nothing to do with acceptance or rejection. A business decision was made.

Before I knew it, the smoke eventually cleared on its' own. After six months, I realized and faced the fact that I actually had been terminated from my previous job, my primary business was not nearly what I had projected, and other business ventures had failed. My confidence, self-esteem and emotions were very low. Because of my experience from my previous job, I felt no desire to ever go back to corporate America. So it was imperative that my business ventures worked especially because of my feelings about corporate America at that time.

As a result of experiencing failure after failure after failure, I ended up succumbing to the idea that no one valued what I had to offer. I felt undervalued by my previous employer, so, the immense emotional toll that was upon me was far worse than dealing with being terminated from a job. Luckily, I was able to shift my mindset about corporate America, the perceived failures and the wrong idea about my services possessing no value.

Journal Question #6

What emotional baggage are you currently carrying with you that you that needs to be released? In what ways are you willing to FORGIVE?

_____

_____

_____

_____

_____

_____

_____

_____

_____

_____

_____

_____

_____

_____

_____

_____

_____

_____

Exercise #7

You have the power to at least lessen the symptoms of sadness due to financial situations. Prepare a budget spreadsheet or graph. List all of your monthly fixed and variable expenses. List the amount of all of the income sources you currently have. Does your monthly income exceed your monthly expenses or vice versa? Whether your answer is yes or no, take a long hard look at your monthly expenses. What services/bills do you absolutely need? What can you do without? Are there any opportunities to minimize the bill on or get a better a rate on services or products? (Page 40)

Budget

Monthly Expense	Monthly Amount Paid	Total Monthly Income
	$	$
	$	
	$	
	$	
	$	
	$	
	$	
	$	
	$	
	$	
	$	
	$	
	$	
	$	
	$	
	$	
	$	
	$	
	$	
	Total: $	

CHAPTER SIX: TEMPORARY SADNESS TO LONG-TERM HAPPINESS

Whether the experience is good or bad, the key is to learn how to accept, adjust, manage and move on. The past cannot be changed, and the only way to truly move on is to embrace that idea. Life is full of peaks and valleys, mistakes and circumstances, which are beyond your control. No person on this planet is exempt from the vicissitudes of life. Life happens! The bus is late and you have an interview. Your car is repossessed during the second week of your new job. Someone you love has been diagnosed with cancer. It is not about how you fall, it is about how you choose to get back up.

I remember in my quest to bring my business to life, going through these valleys of sadness after climbing monumental peaks on my path. Many times I was 'right there' (*right there* is the point where you say, wow, look at what I have accomplished) until something went wrong in the logistics and knocked me right back down to where I started. Yes, it was emotional. Striving for excellence to bring about success can sometimes be a very emotional path. You have to have passion, drive, and most importantly resilience. You must also possess sensors to determine if, and when, it is time to take a break, in order to press forward on to the next day or the next week.

I can recall going through the cycles of sadness to hope and excitement while following my dream. One simple thing that I learned to help me cope with traveling on a road full of surprises and unexpected detours was laughter. Sometimes you just have to walk away and laugh, relax, and clear your mind. Often we do not accept who we are and our expectations of ourselves exceed what is realistically capable at a certain point in time.

Sometimes, acceptance can help you move on to who you are striving to be. Now at first glance, the previous statement may seem contradictory. One may ask, well if I am accepting myself, then why should I strive to be anything more than what I am? Well, my answer to that is this; the only thing constant in the world is change! Every day is a unique day that will never be duplicated, and because of this fact, we are forced to change whether we like it or not. If the adjustments to the ever constant change that we make are positive, we improve ourselves.

The acceptance that I am talking about is having peace with who you are at this very moment. It does not matter where you have been or what you have been through, you are here NOW, and at this very moment, you have a choice in planning who you will become. Every day that you are awakened there is a great element of success in that alone! You are already traveling on the path of success and greatness, which means that you have an unlimited potential at your disposal to identify success and greatness and to master those traits in your character. If you look at many of the successful people in the world today, and throughout history, the one thing that they all have in common is that in their lifetime, they have persevered through undesired outcomes before finally achieving success with their sought after goals and dreams.

It may appear on the outside that the accomplishments successful people have attained seems so effortless, but remember, the truth is that they too have had their share of disappointments, set-backs and more. It is not the accomplishments that make you successful. It is having the ability to rebound with elasticity and resilience after the failures. Successful people know how to find the silver lining in clouds; they know that there are usually positive aspects that can be retrieved from the negative encounters or situations. The ability to get back up after being knocked down, and having the strength to turn your disappointment into 'motivation fuel' to do better on the next attempt is paramount to a successful come back. As you pursue your dreams, you may have to restructure, go back to the drawing board, or identify a new path, but you must never quit.

Journal Question #7

Is there any plan in your life that you have failed to achieve; but if given the opportunity you are willing to give it another try? Why did your plan fail before? What steps would you take to try to make this attempt a success? What would you do differently this time?

_____

_____

_____

_____

_____

_____

_____

_____

_____

_____

_____

_____

_____

_____

_____

_____

_____

Exercise #8

In order to move forward in life, one has to make sure that he or she is not allowing their past to hold them back. This exercise is designed to help you to identify what is holding you back, as well as assist you in the process of making peace with certain situations in your past. On the next three pages you will find two vertical columns. The first column is labeled "The Situation" and the other column is labeled "What did I gain from the Situation". When you write out the pointers from the situation, make sure that you are writing what actually happened and not just from your emotional perspective.   State only the facts about the situation. After reviewing your written pointers from the "What I gain from the Situation", column, ask yourself if taking an inventory of what you have gained has changed your perspective about the situation. (Pages 46-48)

SITUATION INVENTORY

The Situation

What I Gained From the Situation

_____

_____

_____

_____

_____

_____

_____

_____

_____

_____

_____

_____

The Situation

What I Gained From the Situation

_____

_____

_____

_____

_____

_____

_____

_____

_____

_____

_____

_____

SITUATION INVENTORY

The Situation   What I Gained From the Situation

_____   _____

_____   _____

_____   _____

_____   _____

_____   _____

_____   _____

The Situation   What I Gained From the Situation

_____   _____

_____   _____

_____   _____

_____   _____

_____   _____

_____   _____

SITUATION INVENTORY

The Situation   What I Gained From the Situation

_____   _____

_____   _____

_____   _____

_____   _____

_____   _____

_____   _____

_____   _____

The Situation   What I Gained From the Situation

_____   _____

_____   _____

_____   _____

_____   _____

_____   _____

_____   _____

_____   _____

CHAPTER SEVEN: KICK THE STRESSES OF LIFE

So you can't find a job, the rent is due, the car note is past due, and the mafia is after you (well hopefully not the mafia)! Never be afraid of the challenge. Devise a plan. Problems like unemployment can only be addressed with action. Action in this case is 50% mental and 50% physical. If you can move forward with directed actions, then you are truly giving 100%.

The first step in ending unemployment is seeking employment...or is it? There are other creative legal ways to obtain money without punching a clock or sitting in a cubicle for 8.5 hours a day. In some cases, even if you relish in the idea of punching a clock and sitting in a cubicle for employment, you may not have those employment options readily available to you. Competitive job markets, suffering economies, and saturated job fields are a few barriers to finding a viable job.

If you are afflicted with the scenarios listed above within your career, then it is time to sit down and do an assessment of all of your available skills and talents. Simply put, if you have a talent or skill worth paying for, it is possible for you to make a living doing so. After you assess the skills that you have, next you should take inventory of all the tools and resources at your disposal. Discipline yourself and create an environment that allows your talents and skills to work for you.

Once you have identified your talents/skills, and identified the available tools and resources, you may find that you actually have everything that you need in order to successfully launch a business. I did this assessment for my business and was absolutely astounded by the free software that I never paid attention to on my computer. I was also able to make my own high quality commercials by using the video recording feature on my smart phone. Do you see where I am going with this? More on that later!

Journal Question #8

What legal talents do you have that can be, or are already services that people happily pay you for?

_____

_____

_____

_____

_____

_____

_____

_____

_____

_____

_____

_____

_____

_____

_____

_____

_____

_____

_____

Exercise #9

Assess your personal resources. Use the worksheet provided on the next page and fill in the spaces of the five columns labeled Talents, Resources, Connections, Hardware, and Software. This exercise will save you time, money, and in some cases frustration. Your goal here is to jog your memory and list what you already know how to do, what tools/information you currently have, who you know that can help you, what type of electronic/mechanical devices (hardware) you can access, and what software is already contained on the available hardware. (Page 53)

RESOURCE ASSESSMENT

Talents	Resources	Connections	Hardware	Software
Editing Movies	*DVD Burner*	*Michael Anderson*	*Computer*	*Edit Pro*

CHAPTER EIGHT: UNEMPLOYMENT TO EMPLOYMENT

If you are in active pursuance of employment, you may believe that you have to 'pound the pavement' eight days a week, 25 hours a day in order to find a job. Conversely, there are some people who do not believe that they have to do much of anything to land a job. To be honest, looking for work can be like having a job itself, with similar stress levels, deadlines to meet, and the same financial obligations to meet as if you had a job. Why not treat being unemployed like a job? Make a work schedule similar to what you would have within a traditional job setting. However, strive to embrace your creativity and remember, there are many different ways to seek employment. Schedule your activities in efficient yet challenging ways that engage your innovatory abilities.

In a day's work of being unemployed, a task list can include cold-calling from the telephone directory, faxing resumes, posting resumes on internet job boards, canvassing your local area to complete applications in person, and even attending networking events. For tech savvy individuals, you may want to attach your resume to a blog and receive great SEO (Search Engine Optimization)! Whatever activities you choose to elect, make sure that they are diversified and scheduled in a way that is easy for you to stick to. By doing this you will be able to stay organized, maintain a working schedule, and have less risk of burnout.

Exercise #10

While thinking-outside-the-box, brainstorm and list as many ways that you can find out about job opportunities.

1._____

2._____

3._____

4._____

5._____

6._____

7._____

8._____

9._____

10._____

11._____

12._____

13._____

14._____

15._____

16._____

17._____

18._____

19._____

20._____

CHAPTER NINE: A RECESSION LESSON

It is very apparent that recessions can negatively impact an entire nation, and eventually affect global markets, creating a much bigger problem. However, it is what you do in these times of uncertainty that can make the difference between future sustainability and untimely downfalls. Firstly, **ATTITUDE** is the key. Although the awareness of economic crisis and turmoil is inevitable, if you are only focusing on the problem, you and your business will be swept away with the ebb and flow of the issues. Challenge old ideas and shift paradigms to accommodate new circumstances. What can you do in order to survive this moment in history? What can you do that your competitors are not doing right now? What are various ways that you can save money, raise money, and cut costs while delivering above customer's expectations?

So, imagine that you are a determined salmon fighting against the massive downstream flow of water. You desire to continue on fighting with all of your might to move upstream because you have a mission! Big corporations are like salmon swimming upstream against the current, when certain economies and markets are down. It is during tough economic times that corporations may make certain decisions in order to stay afloat, not realizing that their decision will not only propel them through down markets, but establish a whole new level of stable revenue when the economy and markets turn for the better. This is common in the restaurant industry whereas a simple menu item that has become iconic receives a makeover, or a new twist.

Wendy's® offering of a simple, chocolate dairy treat known as the Frosty™ became new and improved simply by offering the Frosty Float, Oreo Frosty Parfait, Strawberry Shortcake Frosty, Carmel Apple Frosty Parfait, and Frosty Shakes featuring new flavors such as Strawberry, Wild Berry, and Vanilla, topped with whipped cream. Even though the Original Frosty™ has a well-established name for itself, and has sold very well throughout the years, the Wendy's® corporate advisors knew that in order to keep a competitive edge that new ideas would have to be mixed with old fashioned favorites. Hungry? It's called DIVERSIFICATION.

I admit, I did laugh out loud the moment that I saw a major grocery store chain offering mortgage services. I instantly thought that if one could get approved for a 30 year mortgage by this grocery store chain, why would they shop for groceries anywhere else, thus creating the faithful, 30+ year returning grocery customer.

More and more businesses are becoming like a one stop and shop. These are places where you can get your car washed, a brand new suit, haircut, financial investment advice, shoes for your baby, and an oil change with free tire rotations while supplies lasts. It is not uncommon to see hair salons that sell hair care, styling products and tools. Most salon owners know that the average person may not afford the opportunity to have hair services every week, so in order to maintain a style, why not sell the tools and products needed to maintain a look between visits? This is convenient for the customers, but a big fat 'Cha-Ching' for the owner. A way to make extra revenue that does not involve trading time for money.

It is simply ingenious for business owners, and an ingenious way to model your efforts. Run your life like a business. Make your decisions as if an entire corporation rests upon your shoulders. Look for ways to diversify your education and skill sets whenever and wherever possible.

Journal Question #9

Using the idea of diversification, what would you do if you had $1,000,000.00?

What decisions would you make in order to continue to live in prosperity?

_____

_____

_____

_____

_____

_____

_____

_____

_____

_____

_____

_____

_____

_____

_____

_____

_____

_____

CHAPTER TEN: SIMPLE TACTICS FOR LIVING SUCCESSFULLY

Keep a clean environment! Wherever you are, make the best out of your situation. If you live in a home, strive to keep it clean and organized. You will be surprised as to how keeping the place where you reside orderly will help to uplift your spirits. In addition, disposing of clutter such as old clothes, papers and items that you no longer need opens up the opportunity for something new to come into your life. Simple fixes such as maintaining your bedroom and bathroom cleanliness is also an important step. If you really think about it, when you wake up in the morning the first thing that you see and experience has the potential to set the tone for your day. Imagine waking up to a room full of clutter, confusion and disarray, it is a reflection of how your life is.

The bathroom is the first place people usually retreat to in the mornings. Trust me, taking a shower in a clean stall, with a clean shower curtain or shower door free of mold and mildew has the ability to start your day off on a positive note, not to mention the immense health benefits!

Journal Question #10

Before writing the answer to this question, please take the time to visualize the specifics of your dream home. If you are already in your dream home, then visualize some positive enhancements that you would like to make. What does your dream home look like? Describe your dream home, room to room, including the landscaping or exterior. What colors are in your home? What adorns the walls? What does it feel and smell like in your dream home? What type/brand appliances and furniture do you have? Have fun visualizing!

Exercise #11

What are some small projects that you can take on in your living space that can change how it feels? Plan to create a powerful living space through de-cluttering, the use of healing colors, displaying inspirational quotes/affirmations, and pictures of you and your family and friends happily enjoying life. Make a plan of action to revamp your living quarters and put it into action! How about changing that shower curtain?

LIVING QUARTERS REVAMP PLAN

1. _____
2. _____
3. _____
4. _____
5. _____
6. _____
7. _____
8. _____
9. _____
10. _____
11. _____
12. _____
13. _____
14. _____
15. _____

CHAPTER ELEVEN: SMALL CHANGES LARGE IMPACT

If you have a little money to supply your basic hygiene needs, then try something new. Sometimes, it truly is the little things that make huge differences in the morale and outlook of life. There are infinite opportunities to revamp and renew your senses and to add interest to your own life beyond the realm of worrying, anxiety and sadness. Instead of purchasing the same products you would normally purchase, be daring and live a little, you won't believe the sheer excitement that is derived from the simple little things. Even if you are on a very tight budget, you can still achieve your own mini bliss within the eye of the storm.

Simple steps can be as easy as buying a new deodorant with a different scent, a new flavor of toothpaste and mouthwash, or a different type of body moisturizer. Even changing the detergents for clothing or dishes can add a dash of sizzle to your life on a budget. Buy a new pillow or a comforting sheet set of bright vibrant colors. Buy an invigorating body wash and body gloves, not only will your skin look nice, but you will feel better. Take a relaxing bubble bath instead of a shower. Make a peanut butter and honey sandwich instead of jelly. Take the scenic route home. Try a new shampoo and conditioner and/or add an uplifting fragrant air freshener to your living quarters. The key here is to do something different than what you would normally do. Remember that each time that you brush your teeth, wash the dishes, walk the dog, or even fold your clothes, that it is a brand new experience every time!

At this very moment, you may not be able to afford to take a vacation, or to own that sports car you may desire, so right now, it is the little simple changes that you can make in your life that will make a tremendous difference in your outlook on life, your situation and your future. Actually take the time to live in the NOW and use what you

have access to, to make every moment you have spectacular!

Journal Question #11

What are 20 minor low cost changes that you can make that can give you a new experience now? (Page 65)

NEW EXPERIENCE NOW LIST

1. _____

2. _____

3. _____

4. _____

5. _____

6. _____

7. _____

8. _____

9. _____

10. _____

11. _____

12. _____

13. _____

14. _____

15. _____

16. _____

17. _____

18. _____

19. _____

20. _____

Exercise #12

Using the 'New Experience Now List', commit to implementing a minimum of three (3) changes per day until you have made all 20 changes. Pay close attention to how you feel about the new experiences and the changes that you have made.

CHAPTER TWELVE: PACKAGING OF SELF: PAPER, PLASTIC OR GUCCI®

First impressions are everything; very rarely do you get the chance to make a second impression. This is why it is very important to have a 'picture perfect' presentation before you attend an interview, business meeting, and in your daily interaction with others in your personal life. First impressions are not just for the world, but they are for you as well. When you look in the mirror, and you think to yourself that you look like a loser, and you step out into the world anyway, that sends a subconscious signal out into the universe. At that moment, you are making a conscious decision to not be in alignment with the vibration of success; which leaves you prone to attract the vibration of defeat that you are sending out. If you look in the mirror and you see a train wreck, you may want to make some adjustments before stepping out into the world! So what if you are only going to the grocery store for a gallon of milk? At least wash your face, remove the rollers ladies, and brush/comb the hair gentlemen. And for crying out loud, please stop wearing pajama pants in public!

Life, luck, and lottery are some examples of situations that have direct impact based upon statistics. You can judge this by the happenings in your own life. The odds that you may "bump into" an old friend, colleague, or a potential client during a 10 minute run to the store are high. How many times have *you* left the house in your less than fashionably demure appearance, and without fail have encountered someone that you know out in public? Did you give that awkward explanation as to *why* your appearance might have been indicative of an old, dirty mop?

When you look good, you feel good. Also, you subconsciously generate a frequency to others matching how you feel. You are also more likely to engage in conversation, make eye contact with others, and even feel compelled to walk up to a stranger to give them a business card. Statistically, you have the power of increasing your chances of positively changing your circumstances if you are always ready to sell and market your most favorite product: YOU!

Journal Question #12

What do you absolutely love? Take a moment to think and write about something that you have tried that you really love. It can be a restaurant, a skin care product, and new vacuum cleaner, etc. Think about how you love this product so much that you have raved to your friends and family about it. You feel very excited about this product/place/thing and what it has done for you! Pay attention to how you feel when you think about the experience. Try to remember the enthusiasm you had when speaking about your experience with others. Now imagine that you were a sales rep for this product that you really love. How would you promote it to friends, family and potential customers? (Page 70)

WHAT I ABSOLUTELY LOVE...

_____

_____

_____

_____

_____

_____

_____

_____

_____

_____

_____

_____

_____

_____

_____

_____

_____

_____

_____

_____

_____

CHAPTER THIRTEEN: BRANDING

The feeling of excitement is what you should have about your accomplishments, skills, aspirations, goals, education, etc., no matter where you are in your life. If you can land an interview, and get a job that you have no experience doing, then you have a talent at self-marketing. The truth is many job positions advertised that require a degree, are in some cases positions that can be successfully learned through on the job training. Therefore, it is not necessarily always education that is needed to get you through the door.

In today's market, employers are looking for what is called a 'good fit'. Being a 'good fit' encompasses a combination of various qualities, not just education, skill set, and professional experience. Having a great personality, or superb soft skills, are huge pluses when marketing yourself for a job. Soft skills are the little things that we sometimes may overlook, such as looking someone in the eye when talking, being courteous and considerate of others, and having good hygiene, etc.

If you are unsure of all of the soft skills that you should have, please take the time to research soft skills by typing 'soft skills' into an internet search engine. You may be missing out on huge opportunities because of something as simple as poor body language or poor communication skills. You could have a Doctorate's degree in a certain field, but if you possess a negative attitude, have problems getting along with people, or you do not have some form of professional etiquette, it may be difficult to find a job and keeping one.

Journal Question #13

What makes you uniquely special? Take the time to think about and write down 20 attributes about you that make you special, and separates you from anyone else that you know. What are your talents, accomplishments, visions, why are you, *you*? (Page 73)

I AM UNIQUELY SPECIAL BECAUSE...

1._____

2._____

3._____

4._____

5._____

6._____

7._____

8._____

9._____

10._____

11._____

12._____

13._____

14._____

15._____

16._____

17._____

18._____

19._____

20._____

Exercise #13

Make a 30 second powerful, declaration commercial. Using **Journal Question #12** 'WHAT I ABSOLUTELY LOVE...' (Page: 70) as a template and some of the attributes to describe yourself, from **Journal Question #13**, 'I AM UNIQUELY SPECIAL BECAUSE...' (Page: 73) write a 30 second commercial about yourself. Remove the product/place/thing from your example of 'WHAT I ABSOLUTELY LOVE!' and with that same enthusiasm, joy and excitement, describe and sell yourself. Really feel the power in your commercial and own it when you speak it aloud! Imagine that the whole world is going to want to know you by the time you finish your 30 second commercial! (Page 75)

30 SECOND POWERFUL DECLARATION COMMERCIAL

Exercise #14

After writing and practicing this commercial, be daring, and take a chance to be extraordinary! Tell no less than 5 people, over the phone or in person, that you are completing an exercise from the *Success Is Spelled with Two C's* guide/workbook, and that you would like to share your personal 30 second commercial with them. Don't worry about how you think the people will react. This is totally about you, not them, and it is a wonderful opportunity for you to solidify who you are by powerfully declaring it to the world through your commercial.

CHAPTER FOURTEEN: CRITICISM: CONSTRUCTION OR DEMOLITION

Think of criticism as a grain of sand on a long, beautiful beach. That grain of sand at any given moment can modestly contribute to a beautiful creation or be swept away by the rising tide. In relation to becoming successful, I had to learn to separate grains of sand. Some grains of sand added astounding beauty to my beach, whereas with other grains of sand, I welcomed the rising tides to whisk them away.

For a long time, I was brainwashed into believing that it mattered what people thought. The beauty in criticism is that it does have its pro's and con's. Thank goodness that one person's opinion does not reflect or represent the opinions of everyone else. Whether you receive negative criticism or positive criticism, any form of criticism is simply an opinion. In my opinion, an opinion is a gathered assessment of a person's subjective reasoning and rationale based on a template of stored ideas and assumptions derived from life experiences.

Looking back throughout history, many of the early philosophers like Socrates and Aristotle were widely criticized about their opinions and teachings, and in some cases, even sentenced to death due to their perspectives and ideas. Today, many of these very same philosophers are vastly studied, quoted and idolized. Many of their ideologies are now accepted and taught within the finest of academic institutions in the world. Do you see where I am going with this?

Journal Question #14

You are your best critic. Embrace this moment in absolute honesty, and write out 10 things that you believe that you are good at doing. Next, write out 10 things that you know that you can improve. What steps do you think you can take to achieve your 10 improvements? (Pages 79-80)

DEEP PERSONAL ANALYSIS

10 THINGS I AM GOOD AT...

1. _____
2. _____
3. _____
4. _____
5. _____
6. _____
7. _____
8. _____
9. _____
10. _____

10 THINGS I CAN IMPROVE...

1. _____
2. _____
3. _____
4. _____
5. _____
6. _____
7. _____
8. _____
9. _____
10. _____

STEPS TO MAKE THE 10 IMPROVEMENTS

_____

_____

_____

_____

_____

_____

_____

_____

_____

_____

_____

_____

_____

_____

_____

_____

_____

_____

_____

_____

_____

_____

_____

CHAPTER FIFTEEN: THIS WORLD OWES YOU NOTHING?

Have you also heard the phrase that "the world owes you nothing"? While speaking with Lifestyle Optimizer, Brandy Edwards of www.brandyedwards.com, I found out that the world most certainly does owe me, and each and every one of us. This concept is not to be misunderstood with the "chip on his/her shoulder" attitude, but more of a re-programming of insufficient or inaccurate data. The universe is an infinite place of boundless ideas, opportunities, wealth and paths. Therefore, the world has the ability to owe you, and give you whatever it is that you are diligently seeking!

Alignment with your true purpose and calling is the key. You would be surprised at what may have once been viewed as hard labor goals, all of a sudden materialize for you so effortlessly, once you are in alignment with the universe. Almost as if the universe has undoubtedly confirmed, that you living out a particular purpose is the very reason that you were able to take your first breath of life, at a specific time and date.

Who would have thought that every win and defeat, struggle and pass, tear of pain or joy, would all lead up to a "moment"? A moment of awe, a feeling of immense gratitude, and adoration of your accomplishments, and a moment when you simply have to be still and quiet--a moment of reflection and recollection, remembering hints and signs along the way that pointed to the once unfathomable level of success that you have achieved.

On your journey, remember to stop to smell the roses. Take the time to enjoy and understand that every moment of your existence was created for you. The sun appeared this morning just for you; or either the life sustaining rain came down this morning just for you. The birds are singing beautifully, and it is all just for you, the *observer*. How ironic is our daily experience when it seems that nothing in our lives is going right and we take the time to look around us, only to find a plethora of aspects in life that are absolutely perfect?

Journal #15

What are some happenings that you have observed, that you have no control over, that are absolutely perfect in your life?

_____

_____

_____

_____

_____

_____

_____

_____

_____

_____

_____

_____

_____

_____

_____

_____

_____

_____

Exercise #15

Create your 'Journal of Proof'! This is a journal (at the end of this guide/workbook pages: 109-119) that you will add dated entries about the AWESOME happenings and wonderful manifestations that take place in your life. Examples can be, finding $1.00, being treated to lunch, receiving an unexpected gift, or even being paid the great words of a compliment. When you feel like things in your life are not going right, or not moving fast enough, pull out this book and turn to the 'Journal of Proof' section and re-read your findings. Your 'Journal of Proof' will serve as a reminder that all things are possible, even if we cannot logically conceive it!

CHAPTER SIXTEEN: SURROUND YOURSELF WITH GREAT PEOPLE

True wealth is not necessarily defined by the accumulation of money. Great people are commodities. When you are surrounded by people of talent, expertise, motivation, resources, etc., you begin to realize how wealthy you are. I can remember a time during my journey of success when I was really striving to promote and brand myself on higher levels. I had no idea at the time that I was practically standing at the door that would inevitably change my life forever. Call it design, or luck, but everything that I needed magically appeared for me, properly and cost efficiently.

I needed a professional website with high-end pictures, make-up, and models. With the expertise and help of my business friends, husband/wife team, make-up artist Brandi Taylor of www.xquisitelooks.com, and photographer and web designer Jason Taylor of www.x-quisitedesigns.com, I was able to establish a professional online presence for under $500.00. I also needed business cards which they handled as well. I needed a promotional DVD for a customer service training contract that I was in the process of bidding on. Thanks to my oldest brother, Global Entrepreneur, and Wealth Coach, Hugh Lee Johnson, (Google him!) and his professional living room studio, I was able to shoot my very first workshop demo DVD for $40.00. (My big brother did not want to accept my money, but I was so grateful for this experience, I wanted to give him something.)

At this point, I thought to myself, what are the millionaires in my industry doing? They are really capitalizing from the use of free social media platforms such as *Facebook, Twitter, Pinterest, YouTube* and more. Although I could have set up all of these accounts myself, I really wanted to focus on honing my skills, writing, obtaining bookings and executing contracts. So, I hired one of my nephews to create my social media pages for my company for $100.00 dollars.

In addition, for my first workshop as a new company, I hired another brother to help me get set-up for the training and gather video footage for $50.00 bucks. All that appeared to be complicated, or maybe financially incomprehensible, proved itself to be simply a mirage from where I am positioned now. An initial investment at a little over $600.00 is what fueled my highly successful journey of becoming what I am today. X+ $600.00 = $1,000,000.00 (X= Resourceful people). I have learned that the value of people around you with a specific expertise is like having a million dollars. Anything is possible! You may find that there are several people who can offer support to your purpose, passion and plan. Perhaps at this point, maybe you should focus your time and energy with people that can help you to achieve your goals. Remember to not take rejection personally because someone in your inner circle may not be able to fully commit to intensive involvement in your goals at this time. The right people can either be right under your nose or just simply a referral away! For those individuals who cannot commit to helping you right now, do not write them off. Periodically keep them posted with your progress and check on their availability.

Exercise #16

Make a list of all the people in your inner circle. Also, make a separate list of your associates and acquaintances. Starting with your inner circle list, write down all talents, resources, or connections they may have. If you do not know what they can offer, simply give them a phone call! Ask yourself how can the people in your inner circle give you support in following through on your goals. Next complete the same tasks with the lists of associates and acquaintances. This exercise will help you to take a bird's eye viewpoint of how people work in your life. (Pages 88-89)

INNER CIRCLE TALENTS AND RESOURCES

Name	Talent	Resources	Connections
Jeniffer Landrom	*Writing*	*Book writing software*	*Knows several editors*

ASSOCIATES/ACQUAINTANCES TALENTS AND RESOURCES

Name	Talent	Resources	Connections

Exercise #17

Find what I call a 'Mental Vision Accountability Partner'. Turn your BFF (Best friend forever) into your MVAP! You and your chosen partner will purposely engage in conversations, and speak on future goals that you both would like to achieve, in the PRESENT TENSE. Speak from the happenings in your life, based on the perspective of you having already accomplished your goals. For example, 'I am giving my old clothes to charity today' becomes: 'I am wiring $500,000 to Africa today for the school I am building there.' Strive to have daily conversations incorporating the goals and dreams and you plan to achieve.

CHAPTER SEVENTEEN: START SOMEWHERE

Whether you see yourself on a map, in a room full of numbered doors, or in a maze, the journey of success can begin anywhere you happen to be in life. 'Somewhere' can be right where you are, at this very moment...

A couple of years ago, I participated in a local event as a vendor. At this event there was a raffle spearheaded by another local business vendor, who agreed to provide free video production and commercial broadcasting on a local cable channel for the raffle winner. On that day, a very deserving business owner won the raffle. I can remember how excited and overcome with emotion this young lady C.E.O. was about being a recipient of this prize. She stated how this prize had come at the right time, as she was struggling to raise proper awareness and financial support for her organization that focused on the literacy success of inner-city youth. Several weeks later, I crossed paths with this same young lady, and when I inquired about her commercial, to my surprise, she stated that not only had no commercial been produced, but the business had not returned any of her calls. I could tell that she was very disappointed.

As we continued to chat, sitting across from each other at a banquet table, I noticed that she had a touch screen 'Smart Phone' similar to one that I owned. Ironically, a week prior, I shot my own commercial video, promoting an upcoming event using my touch screen 'Smart Phone'. I immediately asked, "Why don't you make your own commercial?" She gave me a perplexed look at first, but that changed when I explained how simple and effective of a task it was to use my smart phone's HD quality video camera to record, publish, blast, and track my commercial online.

Sometimes, using what you have and starting somewhere, is the exact remedy to accomplishing major business goals on a shoe string budget. Of course, it also helps to research and gather information before attempting to complete a project that most would pay professionals to do. In my case of novice broadcasting success, I produced a 2 minute video in my living room, using my bedroom lamps, filtered with printing paper to create appropriate lighting. With my smart phone I shot a masterpiece that had far superior visual and audio quality than I expected! Since it was a short video shot with one take, it did not need editing, although the 'App Stores' offer several video editing applications if needed. Once completed, I uploaded the video to my YouTube channel, and copied and shared its' link on several social media sites and generated e-blasts. My video reached hundreds of people and was easily tracked by the YouTube viewer counter, which in my opinion, was effective and offered great marketing flexibility.

It's quite okay to dream big and gaze at the 'big picture', however, keep in mind that if you don't take the time to see the intricacies of the vernacular, you can easily overlook ingenious opportunities and resources to accomplish goals using what you already have, where you currently exist. From what I call 'Big Picture Syndrome", yields the process of setting unrealistic goals that have a tendency to diminish with the same intensity as they were developed. Have you ever experienced a feeling of being overwhelmed and anxious when it came time to develop a plan for your idea? Have you ever experienced how one simple idea can evolve into a multifaceted, confusing concept? Sometimes 'keeping it simple' is the best approach when attempting to follow through. In order to have true, measurable progress, proper planning and practical application are keys for success. Simplicity sometimes enables us to define a clear starting point, and with drive, an idea can potentially be born before the window of enthusiasm and opportunity closes.

So, you have this great idea for a business, product, service, etc. What should you do? Where should you start?

1. **Start with research first.** In order to make sure that you will not be wasting time, money and a significant amount of sweat equity, you will first want to determine if there is a market for your new venture. After all, no matter what your business or idea may be, without customers, a business cannot survive. Great places to start this research can be Google, your local library, marketing firms, and professional/social organizations whose members can be potential customers.

2. **Infrastructure.** If you build on an unstable foundation, your sky scraper will fall. The infrastructure of your business is like the nuts and bolts holding your operation together. It is the legal structure, the business plan, the accounting method, the merchant/banking capabilities, and all other behind-the-scenes inner-workings. Any 'cracks in the foundation' due to poor planning and execution of improper structure, could lead to unfavorable outcomes for your business. If you lack the 'know how' and want information, check with local business development organizations who offer workshops on the subject. In addition, you may also want to find an actual business mentor. Someone who is successfully running their own business. Business mentors can point out pitfalls to avoid, and give you resources so that you don't have to re-invent the wheel.

3. **Think differentiation.** A good case scenario, after your research, would be to find out that there is a high demand for what you have to offer. Now believe you me, in this economy, you may have competitors preparing as diligently as you are to launch similar businesses, concepts and/or products. The unfortunate reality is that not all of these launched businesses will thrive. This means that you will need to set your business apart from the other businesses by over-delivering on customer service, competitive pricing, and creatively thinking-outside-the-box. You will want to effectively and consistently answer the question: "Why would a customer choose my services or products over my competitor's?" The day that you lose sight of that answer is the day that your business can possibly meet its' eminent demise.

4. **Uphold proper business etiquette.** Just because you may have the ability to birth a great business idea does not mean that you have the 'it factor' to keep your business afloat. You are a direct reflection of your business. Understanding that business has its own language, practices, and etiquettes, which if not properly utilized, can negatively impact growth. Simple ideas such as refraining from venting about negative customer interactions via social media, or publicizing personal issues within a business platform, can be the key to building solid credibility and trust amongst potential customers. Striving to have good interpersonal relationships with clients, other businesses owners, and a 'go-the-extra-mile' mentality, creates repeat customers and sows great business Karma! Business circles can be very small, and you never know who's watching, or who

knows who. Remember, a satisfied customer tells 5 people, whereas a dis-satisfied customer tells millions.

These are just a few tips to help motivate you to 'start somewhere'. Starting a business, or running your life as a business may not be easy for some, but it is very rewarding, every step of the way. The easiest part of all is to simply start! Again, it is okay to dream big, but sometimes you have to scale back the flare, the fireworks and the laser show, to a simple, L.E.D. light until a business grows. I know the big picture can be very mesmerizing, but do not forget about the little important steps that it will take to get there. So, be encouraged, you could be holding on to a zillion dollar idea, but you will never know its' true potential unless you 'start somewhere'.

Journal Question #16

How can you "Start Somewhere" in reference to owning a business or restructuring your life? Write out a plan of action that includes your:

- ✓ Mission

- ✓ Short term goals

- ✓ Long term goals

- ✓ Personal talents

- ✓ Resources you identified (software & hardware)

- ✓ Personal behavioral changes

- ✓ People with expertise who can assist you with making your goal

(Page 97)

MY TAKE ACTION PLAN

CHAPTER EIGHTEEN: MENTALLY PREPARE FOR SUCCESS

Have you ever been 'stuck in a rut'? As a man thinks, he becomes. **What you focus on expands!** So why not FOCUS on positive thoughts and ideas? Expose your mind to possibilities that will help you to live your best life. Everything that we expose our minds to is subject to manifest itself, in some way or form, into our lives, whether positive or negative.

Some people believe that we are programmed. Some of us are programmed for success; whereas others are programmed for poverty. I like to use technology as a comparative analogy to how people operate. Software to a computer is synonymous to thoughts to a person. What is the mental software you are running in your mind? If you constantly find yourself consumed with negative thoughts, then you may need to run a 'negative thought virus scan' to clear up the problem!

How can you get awesome results in your life? If you are unhappy with the results of your life, then this is your year for change. Start by changing your tone/vibration/energy. You will want to focus on activities that shift your mind and mood from negativity, to a feeling of emotional gratitude and positive energy. After all, how can you receive the gift that you have been asking, seeking and praying for, if you are not in alignment to receive it?

It is from a positive mindset, where most of your greatest achievements can, and will be accomplished. So, in between your prayers, or meditations, or chants, respectively used to strengthen your faith and spirituality, one the next page, is a list of exercises to strengthen your life muscles in the meanwhile:

1. **Always visualize a favorable outcome for yourself.** See, experience, and embrace the change you want to have. If your goal is to have your own home, visualize yourself writing out your mortgage and utility payments, happily and on time.

2. **Whenever you have a negative thought, immediately replace it with a positive thought.** You can even take it a step further by mentally creating a 'negative thought annihilator' that you can actually imagine using to destroy the negative thoughts. Cool choices can be a galactic hammer, an infinite hole, even a flushing toilet, something that symbolizes removing it from your mind.

3. **Create a mental safe haven.** You will want to complete this exercise during a time that you are really feeling good. You will want to visualize a place that only you are permitted to visit, and that is esthetically pleasing to you, like a park, the mountains, or a river. You will want to enhance this place mentally, by engaging your five senses. What does this place look like? What does it smell like? What do you hear? When you are not feeling emotionally healthy, mentally recall this place.

4. **Think and speak positive words of love, kindness, respect and peace whenever possible.** Words are very powerful. Even when you are speaking about someone else, keep in mind that the words you choose affect *you* first! So make sure that you are harnessing the purposeful power in your life, and in

others, so that you are not affected by the negative intent, connotation and energy that certain words carry. Choose to speak LIFE!

5. **Give back! Be an encouragement to someone else!** Giving back or being a service to someone is a great way to lift your spirits. Sometimes sharing your story with others can be the motivation for them to continue to press forward, and the diversion for your perhaps less than favorable circumstances. Sometimes when you think that you have it bad, there is always someone else who unfortunately may have it worse.

6. **Keep track of all of the positive changes that will take place in your life as a result of these exercises.**

Exercise #18

Write out 7 affirmations on this sheet and then on standard index cards, one in each of the following categories: **spirituality, health, wealth, family, love, success and fulfillment**. Use positive energy words and statements instead of negative energy words and statements. Example: instead of saying 'I am not sick', say 'I am in excellent health'. Carry these cards in your purse, wallet, in the car, or somewhere accessible. Instead of using those precious moments of idle time, as you normally would, perform a powerful, purposeful, activity that will bring great benefit to your life, by simply reading the affirmations on the cards. So, while you are waiting in the salon or grocery store, instead of picking up a tabloid, MP3 player, or your phone, take the time to upload something to your mind that can have positive, long term, tangible benefits.

AFFIRMATIONS

1._____

2._____

3._____

4._____

5._____

6._____

7._____

CHAPTER NINETEEN: THE ART OF BEING STILL

The art of being still is also an action! Sometimes in our lives we need to be still and be quiet for a while, calming the mind and centering self. Sitting quietly, in a quiet location, with your eyes shut, taking deep relaxing breaths is called meditation. Meditation has many benefits such as stress reduction, a positive change in vitality and rejuvenation that encourages a sound peace of mind to name a few.

Meditation has the capabilities to transform your life! Medical research has proven the adverse effects of stress on the body. Meditation is a free tool that does not require any special equipment to experience mental bliss! For novice meditators who may have trouble quieting their minds, a good way to combat the random thoughts that may pop up in your mind is to direct all of your attention to listening to your breathing. Once you begin a daily practice of meditation, you will see how easy it is to work into your schedule and that your mind and body will begin to crave the positive benefits meditation has to offer.

Whether it is 5 minutes, 20 minutes or an hour, the time that you devote to quieting the mind will be well worth it. For more information type 'meditation' into a search engine and you will find a plethora of tips, techniques and types of meditation that can work for you.

One that I like to do before falling asleep is what I call visualization meditation. As I lay in my bed, I visualize what I would like my future to look like. You can visualize the end results of you accomplishing your goals. The goals can be purchasing your dream home, finishing school, meeting your soul mate, having a prosperous career or business etc. I like to do this every night. It inspires enjoyment and excitement about the future and it enables you to align your sub-conscious mind to the universe. When you expose yourself to great thoughts and images in your mind, they have a tendency to manifest in the real world! Have fun creating a beautiful, healthy, loving, life with your power of free will, meditation and visualization!

Exercise #19

Meditate. Find yourself in a quiet, dim or dark location. Sit comfortably in a chair or on the floor with correct posture (spine aligned straight). Close your eyes and rest your hands on your thighs. Begin to relax your body in sections from the crown of your head down to the soles of your feet. Take deep, slow and long inhalations through your nose, expanding your abdomen, and exhale slowing through your mouth retracting the abdomen. 20 minutes a day is a good start, however you can meditate when needed for 2-3 minutes in safe and appropriate locations.

Journal Question #17

Who are you at this very moment? Write out a minimum of three paragraphs expressing who you are. Try your best to provide the most accurate description and intimate portrayal of who you are right now. After you have written about the amazing person that you are, compare this exercise to *Journal Question #1* that you completed. Can you see a transformation? Express what is specifically different about who you are right now. (Pages 106-107)

WHO AM I IN THIS MOMENT…

WHAT IS SPECIFICALLY DIFFERENT ABOUT WHO YOU ARE IN THIS MOMENT…

CHAPTER TWENTY: CONGRATULATIONS!

You have just completed the *Success Is Spelled with Two C's!* guide/workbook. You should be very proud of yourself, for this is truly a monumental accomplishment! You are now on your way to celebrating your life to the fullest! I would like for you to put everything that you learned into action! Review all of your journal entries and exercises. Start fully living out your purpose, connect with people who can help you, and every day, do at least one thing that can bring you closer to completing your goals. Being average is in your PAST, being the embodiment of success is your NOW, and whatever you desire is your FUTURE! Share your experiences of this book/guide and your success stories with at least five other people. Doing this will enhance and empower you and encourage others to seek becoming more successful as well. After all, having a successful circle of people around you has many perks! A successful circle will help foster tremendous personal growth and motivate you to aspire to achieve greater goals. It is my hope that not only did you find immense value from the journal entries and exercises, but that you were able to experience a positive paradigm shift about your existence in this world. I truly hope that you are able to embrace and maintain your new life and all of the infinite possibilities that are available to you. You are a SUCCESS!

JOURNAL OF PROOF

JOURNAL OF PROOF

JOURNAL OF PROOF

JOURNAL OF PROOF

JOURNAL OF PROOF

JOURNAL OF PROOF

JOURNAL OF PROOF

JOURNAL OF PROOF

JOURNAL OF PROOF

JOURNAL OF PROOF

<u>JOURNAL OF PROOF</u>

_____

_____

_____

_____

_____

_____

_____

_____

_____

_____

_____

_____

_____

_____

_____

_____

_____

_____

_____

_____

_____

_____

_____

ABOUT THE AUTHOR

Javay Johnson is a proud, native Detroiter, graduate: Dr. Martin Luther King Jr., Senior High School and Indiana University. For years, her passion has been in helping others to succeed in life. She has reached thousands through her motivational testimony of struggle to success and has been affectionately referred to as "The Life Remodel Specialist". Many people agree that she has an inspiring quality about herself that becomes infectious to those within her presence.

Beyond being an award winning author and motivational speaker, Javay has years of experience working in the Career Services industry for several higher education corporations. Via self-marketing workshops, professional development seminars, and industry-specific resume design, Javay has been responsible for the success of many unemployed individuals becoming gainfully employed.

Javay's experiences have spanned from being an Entrepreneur, Instructor, to a Director on a College's Executive Management team. Her techniques and expertise have also been noted through her contribution to 'Job Search Expert' articles, published within The Detroit News Newspaper 11/13/2008 and 01/01/2009.

Javay is available to facilitate "*Success Is Spelled with Two C's!*" workshops and seminars. Please visit www.JavayJohnson.com for free information, speaking engagements, to order additional copies of "*Success Is Spelled with Two C's!*", to meet Javay and to receive information about her upcoming events.

Made in the USA
Columbia, SC
08 May 2021

37036684R00067